S0-DZP-980

Helping ESL Learners Succeed

by
Kenneth M. Johns
and
Nena Torrez

ISBN 0-87367-684-X
Copyright © 2001 by the Phi Delta Kappa Educational Foundation
Bloomington, Indiana

Table of Contents

Introduction

Teachers need to upgrade the strategies they use to help students who are learning English as a second language. It is crucial to remember that when students are learning the language of instruction while simultaneously learning the content of instruction, teaching them as if they were native speakers of English is both ineffective and unacceptable. This fastback describes several strategies that have been derived from advances in bilingual education and ESL research during the last 20 years.

Before trying to understand how children develop fluency in either a first or second language, it is necessary to differentiate between the terms *language acquisition* and *language learning*. This distinction is important because acquiring a language is quite different from formally learning a language in a classroom.

The only purpose for children to learn a language is to communicate. Because humans need to convey meaning, they grow up speaking language, instead of imitating other familiar sounds in their environment, such as an electric mixer or a Mack truck. Language acquisition in children is an unconscious process in the sense that children are not aware they are acquiring a language and they cannot describe the rules for its use. What they are aware of is a "feel" for the language and that language is used for communicating. In much the same way, children who acquire a second language do so because they need to communicate.

Language learning, on the other hand, requires formal knowledge of explicit rules, forms, and structures. Language teachers in such classes focus on these rules, and they usually believe that the learner will profit from having his or her errors corrected. Error correction supposedly helps the learner master the correct representation of the rule. However, it is important to note that error correction does not help subconscious language acquisition.

So, how does the language acquisition process work? Most current theories assume that every child has an inborn mechanism to learn language. Noam Chomsky (1968) argued that children have an innate capacity to develop grammar based on the linguistic input they receive, and he called this capacity the *language acquisition device* (LAD). More recent research suggests that children's LAD is not limited to grammar, but also includes making sense within the semantic and pragmatic systems of language as well. (Semantics are the shades of meaning words convey. Pragmatics are the social rules that enable language to accomplish real-life purposes.)

Some researchers also add the thought process into this mix. They argue that there is an interactive relationship between language, thought, and social conditions. This view is known as the *constructionist* view of language development and usually is based on the work of the Russian linguist Lev Vygotsky. According to Vygotsky, activity is critical to language development (Bruner 1985). Children learn by doing, and language is no exception. As they interact with others, they use and practice language. Thus language development appears effortless because it is embedded in the everyday process of communication.

In helping young children learn to speak, adults adjust their speech to operate within the children's *zone of proximal development*. Vygotsky's (1978) zone of proximal development is where adults help children to engage in activities that the children could not do on their own. Baby talk and "motherese" use simple words, short sentences, and voice inflections to simplify messages and to highlight important aspects of a message. These alterations in speech provide a form of linguistic scaffolding that facilitates communication.

How does this linguistic scaffolding work? Communication revolves around activities that are meaningful to participants. For example, a child wants a cookie, and language provides a medium for communicating that wish to another. Both participants have a stake in the process. The more proficient partner adapts language to fit the capabilities of the child, raising the stakes by using bigger words and more complex sentences as the child becomes more able. Children acquire more complex language skills through this interaction.

Most current theories are in agreement that children develop language by hypothesis testing, or rule finding, not by repetition, imitation, or mimicry. The evidence to support the "hypothesis testing" theory comes from observing the "errors" children make when they apply the rules they have generated. "Error" has a special meaning in this context. It does not mean mistake, but refers to the forms generated by applying rules that do not take irregularities or exceptions. Errors of this kind are called *overgeneralizations*. For instance, *foots* for *feet* is an example of an error resulting from a systematic effort to make sense out of the rule for plurals. And when children first begin to use past tenses, they often overgeneralize certain words, such as *eated* for *ate* or *goed* for *went*. Researchers know these examples of usage are overgeneralizations of child-generated rules because *goed*, *eated* and *foots* are invented words and not words that children would ever hear from accomplished native speakers.

This view also explains why children are so good at producing sentences they have never heard before. For example, Antonio said, "He nurses at the hospital" and "He fixes sick people." Thus, systematic errors reveal the strategies a child uses to create language, and the rules for each child's system can be inferred from the error patterns the child makes. This also supports the view that children use some type of internal rule system, instead of simple imitation, to govern their acquisition of language.

When learning a language, children first learn what language can do for them. Then they encode this meaning into words and sentences. That is, they learn what functions language can perform. According to Halliday (1975) there are seven categories of language function:

1. *Instrumental:* To manipulate the environment to cause certain events to happen. Used to fulfill needs and desires. (I want to go to the movies.) One-way conversation. Activities: requesting, asking for.

2. *Regulatory:* To enable one to control events or the behavior of others, including approval, disapproval, and setting rules. (Stop hitting me right now! You certainly have gained weight. No throwing spit wads.) One-way conversation. Activities: directing, commanding, convincing, persuading.

3. *Representational:* To allow an individual to communicate information to the world, to convey facts and knowledge. (This is how it is.) Activities: describing, explaining, synthesizing, summarizing, clarifying, responding, retelling.

4. *Interactional:* To get along with others and maintain social communication. Used to relate to others, to establish and preserve ties with family and friends. (Want to play?) Two-way conversation.

5. *Personal:* To allow a speaker to express feelings, emotions, opinions, and views of the world. Used to define oneself. (I think that I need braces.)

6. *Heuristic:* To use language to acquire knowledge, to explore and find out about the world. (Why? What's this?) Activities: hypothesizing, predicting, inferring, considering, asking, reporting.

7. *Imaginative:* To allow the individual to create a personal world, freed from the boundaries of the everyday; using language for sheer pleasure, the language of make-believe. (Let's pretend.)

These language functions are not mutually exclusive. That is, a single sentence might incorporate many functions simultaneously. Nor are they learned in any particular order. Each of the functions is learned when the need arises to do something. Embedded in function is an abstracting and decentering process that involves increasing the distance between the speaker and the subject. Here the language user moves from formulating private thoughts (reflection) to interacting with small, known groups or individuals (conversation) to communicating with relatively anonymous audiences (publication).

Jean Piaget's theory of language development agrees with the above but goes further. According to Piaget, young children go through two developmental stages in their use of language to think and communicate. He calls these stages the *egocentric* and *socialized*. In egocentric speech, the child talks aloud without addressing a listener. In socialized speech, the child is communicating with another (Hennings 1983).

Although the various theories discussed above all describe language functions from different views, each sees language development as the growing ability to fit one's language to a variety of audiences, in varying situations, and for various reasons. And they all support the contention that children acquire language by using it in natural, purposeful, and active ways.

This brief discussion of how first language acquisition occurs serves as a preface to the next chapter, which discusses how second language acquisition occurs.

Second Language Acquisition: The Natural Approach

Because most recognized authorities use the words *language acquisition* and *language learning* interchangeably and without the distinction described above, the term "learning" will be synonymous with "acquisition" from now on.

When referring to language minority youngsters, authorities and educators have used a number of terms with different connotations. However, the preferred and most common term for this population is English Language Learners (ELL). Other terms that might be encountered in the literature and in the schools are: Non-English Proficient (NEP), Limited English Proficient (LEP), Second Language Learner (SLL), Potentially English Proficient (PEP), Students Acquiring English, (SAE), and English as a New Language (ENL).

It should be noted that the labels we use are significant and shape how we respond to the world around us. NEP and LEP are deficit-based terms because they identify students by what they *can't do*, which leads us to serve them in a remedial or compensatory mode. SLL lacks negative connotations; but it can be confusing when referring to native speakers of English learning a new language. Some educators, searching for a way to emphasize language as a resource, rather than a problem, have begun to use such terms as PEP, SAE, and ENL.

Some young children acquire a second language in the neighborhood prior to starting school, but they are the exception. Most non-English-speaking immigrant families cluster in neighborhoods with other immigrants, leaving little opportunity for their preschool children to encounter English-speaking models, except perhaps on television. On entering public school, these children immediately are immersed in a new and largely unfamiliar language environment, where acquiring a second language is necessary for coping in the classroom and on the playground.

However, by the time non-English-speaking youngsters enter school, most have mastered the basic structures and have built up a storehouse of concepts in their primary language. This makes them fairly accomplished communicators. These skills, generally called *common underlying proficiencies*, are carried over and applied to acquiring a second language. To some extent this simplifies acquiring a second language. For example, the Spanish-speaking child comes to school knowing what is meant by *casa*. His only task then is to "discover" the English equivalent, *house*.

This idea has been formalized in a model called the dual-iceberg representation, illustrated in Figure 1. The tips of the dual iceberg represent those obviously different surface manifestations of each language. They represent those elements of both English and the second language that must be acquired independently. Below the surface are the common or shared language proficiencies.

Figure 1. The "Dual-Iceberg" schema for second language acquirers.

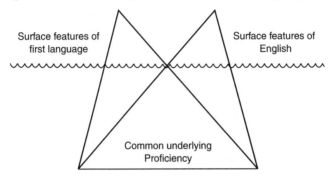

The reason these shared lingual proficiencies are shown below the "water line" is that the average person fails to recognize that many features in one language occur in another. It has been estimated that 80% of the reading and speaking skills taught in English also occur in Spanish. Structures common to both Spanish and English that many teachers do not recognize include sentences that track from left to right and top to bottom, letter/sound correspondence, and order of syntactical elements. In addition, each language has several cognates, or words from the same roots. Similarities between Spanish and English are illustrated in the following sentences:

English:	I	go	to the store	to buy	chocolate.
Spanish:	Yo	voy	a la tienda	para comprar	chocolate.

Similarities also exist between English and other languages, especially Germanic and Romance languages. Thus commonality of language elements supports the proposition that learning a second language is easier than learning the first language.

The *Natural Approach* is one of the most effective communicative approaches. Designed for beginning language students, this method is based on the assumption that, if students have enough comprehensible input, they will teach themselves how to talk.

According to Krashen and Terrell's (1983) theory of language acquisition, a learner goes through four stages of development in pursuing his quest for second language fluency: Pre-production, Early Production, Speech Emergence, and Intermediate Fluency.

Stage I: Pre–Production: "The Silent Period"

In this first stage, or "silent period," of second-language acquisition, the learner is concerned with receiving speech, rather than speech production. Production of speech in a new language requires substantially more cognitive effort than reception because the learner usually must translate the message into his primary language before responding. The following illustrates the cognitive process required for speech production:

English speaker: How much do two beers cost?

Learner:

1. (Conceptualizes English meaning.) How much do two beers cost?
2. (Mentally translates into first language.) Cuánto cuestan dos cervezas?

3. (Mentally forms answer in first language.) Cuestan
   dieciséis pesos para dos cervezas.
4. (Mentally translates answer into second language.) Two beers cost 16 pesos.
5. (Speech response.) Two beers cost 16 pesos.

For most beginning second-language learners, the
"translation" process becomes overwhelming because
they become preoccupied with the form to the neglect
of communication. But in the "silent period" stage, there
is time for the learner to concentrate on comprehending messages in the new language. Word and sentence
formation are ignored for the time being because they
interfere with understanding. This is a time for getting
acquainted with a new system of speech sounds,
rhythm, and intonation. And it is a time for associating
a new vocabulary with familiar concepts in one's first
language. It is also the place where such nonverbal language components as body language and gestures are
absorbed.

Since the focus at this stage is on comprehension, the
learner's responses are usually nonverbal ones, such as
pointing, touching, and nodding.

Exposure to natural communication in the second
language is necessary for the subconscious language
processes to work. The richer and more frequent the exposure, the faster the acquisition process takes place.

However, mere exposure is not enough. The acquirer needs to comprehend the message in a social and
meaningful context. Comprehending must come before
speaking. Krashen and Terrell (1983) call this *compre-*

hensible input, which means that the learner acquires an understanding of the message but does not focus on or analyze the form of the input. Understanding does not mean recognizing every word or interpreting every syntactical structure; instead, it means to understand the essence of what is being communicated. Language containing structures that are not "known" can be understood by using context, extra-linguistic information, and one's own knowledge of the world.

For speech to have "comprehensible input," it must contain a real message, and there must be a need for the message to be communicated. Speech that does not contain a real message and that is presented only for the practice of some rule may be useful for some learning purposes, but it will not contribute to language acquisition.

Another important hypothesis for language acquisition is the *affective filter hypothesis*. This hypothesis relates to emotional variables, including anxiety, motivation, and self-confidence. Learners in a less than optimal affective state develop a filter, or "mental block," preventing them from using input for further language acquisition. Thus, if they are subjected to embarrassment, humiliation, or other negative responses when trying to learn a second language, the input is not likely to enter the language acquisition device (see page 8). On the other hand, small increments of language, available to the learner when they are embedded in comprehensible input, are very accessible in non-threatening, low-anxiety situations. A positive affective context increases learning. Krashen and Terrell (1983) refer to the affective component of language acquisition as an *affective filter*, a kind of emotional barrier to language learning that must be lowered if acquisition is to take place. Even though the affective filter is somewhat difficult to define operationally, most teachers understand that a congenial and jovial environment promotes learning.

The affective filter hypothesis is related to the *effect of personality*. A person with strong self-esteem is better equipped than a person with a low self-concept to withstand some of the embarrassment that naturally occurs when he makes language errors. That is, if one is outgoing, the likelihood of becoming involved in situations where he can use and practice new language is greatly enhanced. Thus an outgoing person is more likely to move through the stages of second language acquisition at a much faster rate than a shy person. One piece of evidence for this effect comes from recent research that suggests a person's ability to use a second language is improved after taking a glass or two of wine. The hypothesis is that the person's inhibitions are lowered, making the person more willing to take risks involved in trying out a new language. Of course, this phenomenon is not appropriate in a school setting.

One strategy widely used by teachers with students who are in the silent period is the Total Physical Response technique (TPR). With this approach, the instructor gives and executes a command, such as "Touch your nose!" and the class responds as a group by executing the command. Later, the same kind of command can be given to individual students. With TPR, no verbal response from the student is expected; only execution of the command is required.

Speech presented during this pre-production period typically is language used in routine classroom management, such as "Stand up," "Take out your book," "Line up at the door." Other language used includes names of people close to the student, names of body parts, common classroom objects, and articles of clothing. Introductory TPR activities also might include statements that cover size, color, number, and location: "Put three, big, yellow pencils on the desk."

Pictures and other visuals can be used in much the same way as classroom objects. The instructor describes what is in a picture or in a group of pictures placed on a slot-chart and asks the group to identify certain objects. Pictures allow the teacher to expand language input beyond the immediate classroom. For example, pictures can be used from a store or a zoo. Language input with a group of ELLs using an animal theme might sound like this:

Here's a new picture. What do we see in the pictures? (Without waiting for a response) A turtle, a buzzard, and a rabbit. Here's the turtle (pointing). Here's the buzzard. And here's the rabbit (pointing again).

Who wants to hold the picture of the turtle, the buzzard, and the rabbit? (Hands up.) Nina. Nina is holding up the picture of the turtle, the buzzard, and the rabbit. Nina, point to the picture of the buzzard. (If Nina does not understand "buzzard," the teacher points at the buzzard and repeats, "buzzard.") Nina, give the picture of the turtle, the buzzard, and the rabbit to Jose. (Gives picture to Jose.)

Who has the picture of the turtle, the buzzard, and the rabbit? (Jose) Jose, point to the turtle. Show Nina the picture of the turtle.

In this exercise the instructor's primary objective is identification of particular animals or English vocabulary development. A second objective is to reinforce the concept of possession: "Give the picture to. . . ."

Careful consideration should be given to the language of the instructor. First, there is no attempt to use the students' first language or any kind of a translation approach. The whole lesson is conducted in English. Conceptually, the children "know" these animals from their primary language experience, so they need to understand only the English equivalents. Second, when teaching second-language learners, a helpful native speaker, such as the instructor, uses the following strategies and contextual support:

- Slower rates of speaking.
- Clear articulation.
- Simple vocabulary.
- Repetition and rephrasing.
- Gestures.
- Visuals.
- Paraverbal expressions.

Third, the language is natural. The teacher chooses "here's" instead of "here is" because the children are more likely to encounter the contraction form in informal conversational situations, such as on the playground.

TPR should be used until all the children can understand the important words that are used daily in the classroom. Most children quickly acquire enough vocabulary at the oral recognition level to follow the teacher's commands without the students producing a single word in English. And they have acquired some sense of how simple sentences are sequenced without any formal grammar lessons.

This pre-production stage may last from a few hours to several months. Generally, children need one to two months before they are ready to advance to the next stage of language acquisition, early production.

Stage II: Early Production

Speech emerges slowly but naturally at different rates for different children. At the early production stage, children move beyond listening comprehension and begin to communicate using one or two words. This stage follows the theory of one-word, two-word, three-word development in primary language acquisition. Usually these first words and phrases are those that the acquirers have heard frequently enough to feel confident in producing. The first speech produced usually consists of such high-utility words as "yes," "no," "glass," and "lunch" or such routine expressions as "How are you?" and "Thank you."

According to Cummins (1981), when children begin to produce speech, they quickly develop *Basic Interpersonal Communicative Skills* (BICS) from their playmates, the media, and their daily experiences. BICS are the language skills required for face-to-face communication, where interactions are context-embedded — the language of necessity, the language of need. For example, a child may be a newcomer to a classroom where all socialization and instruction is conducted in English and no one in his room knows his primary language. Driven by basic human needs, such as going to the bathroom, this child will be quick to learn the phrase, "Can I go to the bathroom?" as well as the social conventions (context) that go with it, such as raising one's hand to ask permission.

Because children acquiring a second language need to get things done, BICS and motivation to learn these skills go hand in hand. Motivation may be *instrumental* or *integrative*. Instrumental motivation is what drives a person to acquire a second language for reasons of survival in day-to-day living. The adult learner is motivated to master English in order to communicate with people on the job and in the community — the merchant, the banker, the local bookie. Likewise, the child must learn to function with his peers in a school and community setting.

Integrative motivation is less compelling. It is the desire to belong — to be identified as a member of the group. Most youngsters in English as a Second Language (ESL) classes exhibit integrative motivation. They do not need to learn a new language for survival reasons, but they do have a strong drive to be accepted by their English-speaking peers. Teachers should capitalize on this drive when working with ELL students.

Another factor that affects early production is the age of the learner. Even though it generally is assumed that children learn second languages better than adults do, older children do better in achieving second language proficiency than younger ones because older children have a further developed conceptual base in their primary language as a result of literacy skills and previous schooling. Learning a second language for them is a matter of restating first-language concepts and ideas that already are firmly ingrained. Unlike younger children, who face the more difficult task of having to learn basic concepts in a new and unfamiliar language, older students need to learn only new labels.

However, when comparing adult to child proficiency, it is important to look at the aspect of pronunciation. Children who learn their second language before puberty do, in fact, acquire native-like pronunciation, unlike adults, who usually speak a second language with an accent.

At the early production stage, it is not necessary that children pronounce all words precisely unless a mispronunciation interferes with meaning. Though humans have the potential of reproducing the sounds of any language in the world, from infancy the sounds unique to any language become internalized in a child's cognitive system through repetition and reinforcement. Those sounds that do not occur in a child's primary language become harder to reproduce as the child grows older. After the age of about seven, the vast majority of people are never able to reproduce certain sounds exactly as a native speaker would. The older person acquiring a new language substitutes sounds he or she "knows" to approximate those unique to the second language. That is why adults, such as Arnold Schwarzenegger and

Antonio Banderas, who are fluent in English, have heavy accents. Preoccupation with precise pronunciation detracts from the acquirer's primary objective of communicating meaning and should not be emphasized if the affective filter is to be lowered.

Phonetic reproduction problems can best be illustrated by looking at common mistakes learners make. For instance, it is not uncommon for Spanish-speaking acquirers to intermix the <sh> sound (as in sheep) with the <ch> sound (as in cheap). This learner might say, "The farmer has two cheap," when he means, "The farmer has two sheep," or "The candy was sheap," when she means, "The candy was cheap." Such examples can and should be ignored by teachers as long as what the learner is saying can be understood from the context.

However, sometimes correction of pronunciation is necessary. For instance, Asian learners often switch the <l> and <r> sounds. The acquirer may say, "I rike flied lice," when he means, "I like fried rice." This mispronunciation may confuse the message and subject the learner to ridicule by his peers. In this situation, correction of pronunciation is appropriate. The "rike" and the "flied" may or may not cause any communication problems, but the teacher needs to point out the lexical difference between "rice" and "lice."

There are several strategies a teacher can use to evoke one- or two-word responses. For example, the teacher may ask, "What is this?" Or she may begin a statement and indicate by voice intonation that the child should complete the statement: "Is this a book? No, it's a [pencil]."

Questions requiring a dichotomous answer — such as yes-no, here-there, and either-or — also are appropriate at this level. Here the children are given an opportunity to say some of the words they can recognize. The easiest way to ask these types of questions is to embed them in the context of the interaction. For example, the teacher has several stuffed animals: a rabbit, a bear, a mouse, a cat, etc. She chooses the bear and says, "Is this an animal?" [Yes.] "Is this a bear or a mouse?" [Bear.] The teacher then throws the bear to the student farthest from her and asks, "Is the bear here or there?" [There.]

The transition from the pre-production stage to the early production stage should be gradual and spontaneous. The teacher should encourage and guide the student to produce language but should never force performance.

Stage III: Speech Emergence

At the third stage, speech emergence, children begin to speak in simple sentences. At this stage, the emphasis shifts from language reception to language production in the form of simple sentence patterns and short dialogues. At this point it is helpful for the child to memorize specific, high-utility patterns without necessarily knowing the exact meanings of each of the individual words. A dialogue might proceed as follows:

A. What is your name?
B. My name is Enrique. What's yours?
A. My name is Maria. Where do you live?
B. I live on Oak Street. Where do you live?
A. I live down the street. What are you going to do?

B. I'm going to eat lunch. What are you going to do?
A. I'm going to eat lunch, too. Let's go together.

At this stage, the teacher can begin to use "how" and "why" questions when interacting with learners. These types of questions require the student to respond in whole sentences, rather than one- or two-word responses. Following are examples of using "how" and "why" questions:

Teacher: Why is the boy wearing that hat? (football helmet)
Student: He is going to play football.
Teacher: How did the honey get into the jar?
Student: Pooh Bear put it there.

The above examples show how the learner continues to receive "comprehensible input" while at the same time engaging in enjoyable activities. Children's intonation and pronunciation improve, their vocabulary expands, and they produce longer and longer sentences.

In addition to BICS, which students have already begun to master at this stage, they need to develop Cognitive Academic Language Proficiency (CALP) (Cummins 1981). CALP provides the language skills required for academic achievement in the classroom and is quite different from the basic skills necessary for everyday communication. If teachers fail to recognize this difference, they may erroneously assume that children have acquired sufficient proficiency in English to succeed in a classroom where only English is used, when in fact they have not.

Since children of school age are beginning to develop reading and writing skills (CALP) at this stage, educators have begun to understand that language learning is most meaningful when it is tied to content instruction. A teaching approach that has been successful in helping individuals master school content is Sheltered English or Specially Designed Academic Instruction in English (SDAIE), the preferred term. SDAIE has four goals: that students learn English, learn content, practice higher-level thinking skills, and advance their literacy skills. SDAIE applies to all aspects of instruction, including planning, classroom management, lesson delivery, and assessment. It is useful for intermediate second language speakers and as a bridge for students about to make the transition to all-English classrooms.

Snow, Met, and Genesee (1989) suggest that language development is facilitated when it is combined with content area instruction for the following reasons:

- Cognitive development and language development are inextricably tied, especially for young children.
- School subjects are what children need to talk about in school, so content area provides both the motivation and the opportunity for meaningful communication.
- Tying language development to the content area allows students to develop the kind of language that is used in school.

According to Johns and Espinoza (1992), involving language minority students in *cooperative learning* groups in the mainstream classroom is a strategy teachers have used successfully. Working cooperatively on assignments and projects with native speakers of English increases the opportunities ELLs have to hear and produce language and to negotiate meaning with others. Cooperative learning activities provide a nonthreatening atmosphere in which ELLs feel accepted and more confident about themselves, thus raising their self-esteem. Also, friendships develop among students of different backgrounds.

As we have discovered, ELLs learn English by interacting with their peers in the classroom and on the playground. In school they learn functional words and phrases, such as "Where's the bathroom?" or "It's my turn!" Cooperative grouping takes this process a step further by requiring children to use words within the context of an academic task (CALP). They come to understand and use the specialized vocabulary necessary to successfully complete the group task. They feel more comfortable taking risks with language in a small group of peers than in a large whole-class setting. They become involved in the culture of the classroom as part of a group working toward a common goal, and everyone has responsibility for achieving the group's goal.

Cooperative grouping allows children to get to know each other in ways that do not happen in a whole-class setting. When left to their own devices, children tend to pick their friends from their own social or linguistic group. However, cooperative grouping provides students the opportunity to work with those they may never have considered interacting with. In such a setting, the likelihood of their becoming friends increases. For this reason, the teacher should make sure that language minority students are represented in each group whenever possible.

Stage IV: Intermediate Fluency

At the intermediate fluency stage, the student engages in spontaneous dialogue and composition. Here the emphasis is on vocabulary development in both languages and learning more sophisticated syntactical patterns. Also, colloquialisms and idiomatic expressions are introduced at this level. At this point the student begins to "think" in the second language, instead of conceptualizing in the native language and then translating into the target language.

At this stage there are many activities that can be used to promote fluency in a second language. Again, the important thing to remember is that the activities need to stress speech production, rather than focus on grammatical form or correctness.

Verbal games are a highly motivating way to learn language in a relaxed atmosphere. In mastering the game, students acquire new vocabulary and use it as they interact with one another. Action-type games, such as "Simon Says" or "Mother, May I?" are especially effective in generating spontaneous speech production in English.

Another good language-learning activity is to engage children in talking about themselves, their desires, preferences, abilities, or feelings. Following are examples of how a teacher can initiate conversations or discussions in which students talk about themselves:

Desires: Halloween is coming up. You need to think of what you want to be, what costume you want to wear. On Halloween you want to be a _____. Why?

Preferences: I will give you several choices, and I want you to decide which you prefer. We are going to plan a class party, and you need to decide what we are going to do and what we are going to eat. Which do you like best, dancing or games? What kind of dancing? Why? Which games? Why? Pizza or dessert? What kind of pizza? Why? What kind of dessert? Why?

Abilities: I will tell you how to do something. Some things I tell you will be true and some will be false. You need to decide if I really know how to do it. Whatever you decide, you must tell me why you decided what you did. [Teacher gives directions and ingredients for making a cake using, among other ingredients, pickle juice, chili powder, and super glue.]

Feelings: I will give you a "feeling" word. When I do this, I want you to think of where you are when you have this feeling. I am (teacher mimes "sick to my stomach") when I am _____. (Galyean 1977)

Researchers in the area of second language acquisition have discovered that the process is quite complex because language learning is a multifaceted problem-solving activity. Much as they would approach any problem, people approach language learning using the information and abilities they already have. It is the teacher's role to facilitate this process by providing activities and experiences that lend themselves to the principles of second language acquisition and the stages children go through when learning to become fluent in English.

Working with Parents and Other Caregivers

Caregiver refers to those responsible for child rearing in the home. They include parents, older siblings, relatives, extended family, and babysitters. Caregivers obviously have played a key role in the child's acquisition of his native language. Their role in the child's acquisition of English depends on their own fluency (if any) and on their attitude about having their children learn English in the first place.

Some non-native English-speaking parents, who recognize the economic and social benefits of knowing the dominant language in American culture, go to great efforts to speak only English to their children at home if they can. This is unfortunate. By failing to use their native language at home, they virtually extinguish it in their children; and the opportunity for their children to become truly bilingual after a few years in school is lost.

There is ample evidence to show that the use of the native language in the home is not a handicap to a child's acquiring English. On the contrary, research tells us that having a rich language experience in one's primary tongue has a beneficial effect on learning a second language. The point is, the more the learner uses language — any language — the quicker he or she learns English. So teachers should encourage the use of the native language in the home.

Schools should inform limited- or non-English-speaking caregivers of some of the things they can do to support their children's acquisition of English. Caregivers should be encouraged to tell stories, folk tales, sayings, riddles, and jokes in the child's native language. Also, caregivers can share with children records, photos, letters, and artifacts from their native culture. These objects stimulate immediate language use and concept formation, which facilitate "comprehensible input" when beginning to learn English. Caregivers can read stories from native-language children's books and make these books and other printed material available for browsing. In addition, selective use of radio, TV programs, and movies in the child's native language can augment language development. These media can serve as springboards for discussions on issues affecting the family and can help develop critical thinking skills, which will be useful later when the child becomes more proficient in English.

Schools can encourage caregivers to have their children share aspects of their native language and culture, such as foods, traditional celebrations, music, dance, and clothing. Opportunities to share their cultural heritage foster children's self-esteem and reduce their "affective filter."

The Role of Technology in Helping ELL Children

Over the past decade there has been a dramatic increase in various media and computer applications designed specifically to address the needs of English language learners. University language departments are developing new technologies for the curriculum on a regular basis, and information technology offers new possibilities for rich content, expanded assessment capabilities, and immediate feedback. Many school districts across the nation are creating special magnet high schools where technology, international studies, and second languages are emphasized. Technology is becoming a bigger part of both in-class and home study as computer-assisted instruction and interactive media supplement the traditional use of audio and films.

The use of information technology to further enhance the environment for second language learners involves a technology plan that addresses key issues. One of the first steps in technology-assisted instruction is to decide which medium is the most appropriate one for the language skill(s) to be developed during a particular period of time. Some technologies lend themselves better to the acquisition of certain language skills than do others.

Computer-Assisted Instruction and E-Mail

Computer-assisted instructional (CAI) programs are ideal for fostering reading and writing skills in the target language. CAI can be used by groups or individual students in a classroom or media center or over local or long-distance computer networks.

E-mail provides a real form of communication between students. Whether the message arrives from a classmate on campus or originates on the other side of the globe, the use of such a real form of communication motivates students to read that message and, in turn, to respond in writing.

Programs that use fill-in-the blank, multiple-choice, and true/false questions help students to write at the word level. Databases and spreadsheets provide students with practice in retrieving information and problem-solving skills.

Word processors are ideal for compositions or free writing, and some word processors are bilingual and provide on-line assistance with dictionaries, spell checkers, and grammar helps. When technology is used interactively among students, cooperative writing activities are strong motivators to help students develop writing skills. With a basic word-processing program, students can write short articles and compile and edit a newspaper based on their classroom exchanges. The use of such text-based applications is just one of the many possibilities for extending language learners' potential.

Some CAI programs enhance word recognition through cloze activities (every nth word deleted), anagrams, jumbled words, and so on. To practice reading at the sentence level, computer programs provide practice in ordering words within a sentence, text reconstruction, or ordering sentences within a paragraph. Other CAI programs provide articles or stories as reading comprehension passages with accompanying word helps and comprehension questions at the end of the selection.

Testing is another area where CAI is useful. Computer-assisted testing now provides a more comprehensive, fast, and accurate way of testing student language skills, other than speaking skills. Students also can test themselves by using CAI programs.

Interactive Audio

Audio capabilities can be added to personal computers, using either audio boards or a CD-ROM with microphones for input and headphones for output. And by connecting a special tape recorder to the computer, interactive audio provides multiple possibilities to teach and test active listening skills. In computer-assisted audio, the printed screen is combined with sound for the acquisition of listening and speaking skills, as well as reading and writing skills.

An interactive audio program allows students to create dialogues and to practice them with other students. Other task-based speaking activities also can be used effectively with interactive audio programs.

Video

The visual component of video is especially useful for cultural and paralinguistic information. Regular linear video is most useful for developing listening skills and creating cultural awareness. Video with target-language subtitles also can serve in developing reading skills. Video enables students to observe the dress, food, climate, and gestures of the target culture.

When the power of a computer is added to video so that there is instant access to sound, vision, and text, the resulting interactive video system can provide practice in all of the language skills. Students' skills in listening and reading, as well as in writing and speaking, can be greatly enhanced when these latter options are available on an interactive compact disc (CD) program. Given that language is an expression of culture, cultural aspects of the video segments can be highlighted using the CD program to provide a better context for communication.

Videotapes or interactive CDs also can provide excellent listening comprehension activities, provided that a good listening guide is prepared for the students. Depending on the language level, students listen for just the main idea of a segment, or they listen for specific facts in the video program.

The Internet

The number of sites that provide information to support second language learning and to emphasize the importance of a second language is growing as fast as the Internet itself. There is no need to make a comprehensive list of such websites. However, one of these destinations will be cited as a good example of an effective means to link and filter the growing amounts of information in this field.

Dave's ESL Cafe is one of the most popular ESL sites (possibly *the* most popular ESL site) on the World Wide Web. Its creator, Dave Sperling, is an outstanding ESL professional who is using the Web in imaginative ways to enhance English language instruction for teachers and students.

The on-line learning/teaching section of Dave's ESL Cafe includes the *Help Center,* where students can consult an international team of ESL/EFL teachers; the *Quiz Center,* offering many on-line quizzes that are scored immediately; the *Quote Page,* which contains quotations, proverbs, and humor; and the *Idiom Page,* the *Phrasal Verb Page,* and the *Slang Page,* which offer definitions and sample sentences for idioms, phrasal verbs, and slang expressions, respectively. The global communication section includes the *E-Mail Connection Pages,* where students and teachers can meet; the *Message Exchange,* for both students and teachers; the *Discussion Center,* which contains a series of forums on such topics as current events, food, and movies; the *ESL Address Book,* which includes the addresses of students, teachers, schools, and publishers; and *Chat Central.*

The resources and information section consists of the *Idea Page,* the *Search Page,* and the *Job Center,* which includes the *Job Links Page,* the *Job Discussion Forum,* the *Job Wanted Forum,* the *Job Offered Forum,* and *ESL Job Chat.* You can go to all of the pages from this Cyber Cafe's main page (http://www.eslcafe.com).

With technology-assisted instruction, there are changes in both educator and student roles. Students are given more responsibility for their own learning, while the educator serves as a guide and resource expert who circulates among students, working individually or in small groups.

The new technologies offer many possibilities to the second language learner. The effectiveness of these technologies depends on appropriate use by informed educators. Neither textbooks nor technology can replace the live, unprogrammed feedback and interaction of the language teacher.

The English-Only Controversy

Because of widespread voter approval of English-only laws, many politicians continue to uphold the popular notion that English is the one acceptable medium of communication and instruction at school. This is the case even though an overwhelming preponderance of the research supports bilingual education as the ideal way for ELLs to master curricular content and English proficiency skills.

Although the exclusive use of English in teaching ELLs has come to be seen as a natural and commonsense practice that can be justified on pedagogical grounds, it is rooted in a particular ideological perspective, rests on unexamined assumptions, and serves to reinforce inequities in the broader social order. Evidence from research and practice suggests that the rationale used to justify English-only in the classroom is neither conclusive nor pedagogically sound. Therefore, to effectively serve the total ELL population, it is necessary for all teachers of language minority students to at least familiarize themselves with the nature of alternative programs that are designed to help school children master English. Bilingual programs, ESL programs, and English-only programs are described below.

Bilingual Programs

All bilingual programs use the students' home language, in addition to English, for instruction. These programs are implemented most easily in districts with a large number of students from the same language background. Students in bilingual programs are grouped according to their first language, and teachers must be proficient in both English and the students' home language.

While bilingual education generally is defined as any school program that uses two languages, the coordinated, developmental bilingual approach emphasizes being fully proficient in all facets of both languages. That is, the students should be able to listen, speak, read, and write in both languages. Realistically, this has not been the goal for most K-12 bilingual schools in the United States.

More commonly in the United States, we use "bilingual program" to describe a program that provides literacy and content in the primary language while building English fluency, with the goal of all instruction eventually being conducted in English. These programs really are "transitional bilingual programs," as their ultimate goal is to transition all students into English-only classes. One of the down sides of these programs is that they are not designed to preserve and develop

41

students' primary language while they acquire English as a second language.

Early-exit bilingual programs are designed to help children acquire the English skills required to succeed in an English-only, mainstream classroom. These programs provide some initial instruction in the students' first language, primarily for the introduction of reading, but also for clarification. Instruction in the first language is phased out rapidly, with most students mainstreamed by the end of the first or second year. The choice of an early-exit model may reflect community or parental preference, or it may be the only bilingual program option available in districts with a limited number of bilingual teachers.

Late-exit programs differ from early-exit programs primarily in the length of time that English is used for instruction. Students remain in late-exit programs throughout elementary school and continue to receive 40% or more of their instruction in their first language, even after they have been reclassified as fluent-English-proficient.

Two-way bilingual programs (also called developmental bilingual programs) group language minority students from a single language background in the same classroom with language majority (English-speaking) students. Ideally, there is a nearly 50/50 balance between language minority and language majority students. Instruction is provided in both English and the minority language. In some programs, the languages are used on alternating days. Others may alternate morning and afternoon, or they may divide the use of the two languages by academic subject. Native English speakers and speakers of another language have the opportunity to acquire proficiency in a second language while continuing to develop their native language skills. Students serve as native-speaker role models for their peers. Two-way bilingual classes may be taught by a single teacher who is proficient in both languages or by two teachers, one of whom is bilingual.

ESL Programs

ESL programs are likely to be used in districts where the language minority population is very diverse and represents many different languages. ESL programs can accommodate students from different language backgrounds in the same class, and teachers do not need to be proficient in the home languages of their students. Although schools with a large number of ESL students may have a full-time ESL teacher, some districts employ an ESL teacher who travels to several schools to work with small groups of students scattered throughout the district.

Pull-out ESL programs generally are used in elementary school settings. Students spend part of the school day in a mainstream classroom but are pulled out for a portion of each day to receive instruction in English as a second language. The ESL resource center is a variation of the pull-out design, bringing students together from several classrooms or schools. The resource center concentrates ESL materials and staff in one location and is usually staffed by at least one full-time ESL teacher.

The ESL class period generally is used in middle schools. Students receive ESL instruction during a regular class period and usually receive course credit. They may be grouped for instruction according to their level of English proficiency.

English-Only Programs

English-only programs provide neither instruction in the native language nor direct instruction in ESL. However, instruction is adapted to meet the needs of students who are not proficient in English.

Sheltered English or content-based programs group language minority students from different language backgrounds together in classes where teachers use English as the medium for providing content-area instruction, adapting their language to the proficiency level of the students. They also may use gestures and visual aids to help students understand. Although the acquisition of English is one of the goals of sheltered English and content-based programs, instruction focuses on content, rather than language.

Structured immersion programs use only English and, by design, there is no explicit ESL instruction. As in sheltered English and content-based programs, English is taught throughout the content areas. Structured immersion teachers should have strong receptive skills in their students' first language and have a bilingual education or ESL teaching credential. The teacher's use of the children's first language is limited primarily to clarification of English instruction. Most students are mainstreamed after two or three years.

Conclusion

Much research has been done in the past 20 years on how language learning takes place. Among the central findings is that there is a certain order in which language structures are acquired and that this occurs whether a person is learning a first, second, or third language. This "universal order" differs from the grammatical sequence traditionally used by foreign language teachers.

In acquiring a second language, children go through four stages: pre-production, early production, speech emergence, and intermediate fluency. Children move through these stages at their own pace. Forcing language production delays or retards progress. Fluency develops gradually as a subconscious process. Formal learning of grammatical structure comes later.

In order for second language acquisition to occur, three conditions must be met. First, the learner must perceive a need to communicate in the new language. Second, the acquirer must receive "comprehensible input." Third, the comprehensible input must occur in a low-anxiety environment.

The role of the teacher in second language acquisition is to structure an environment in which the acquirer finds it necessary to communicate. The teacher should use a variety of techniques so that the message is understood. Above all, the teacher should take an interest in the child's first language and culture and should accept all attempts made by children to communicate.

Caregivers should provide an environment rich in language experiences, where children can develop in English and their native language and grow intellectually. They also should cooperate with the school in its efforts to help their children acquire a second language.

Technology has taken on an ever-increasing role in both primary and second language instruction and will continue to do so at warp speed. Since technology lends itself well to programs designed to accommodate English language learners, it is critical that teachers and caregivers become well-acquainted with and take full advantage of this valuable resource.

To become effective mentors for English language learners, teachers and caregivers must be thoroughly familiar with all the program options and approaches available to serve language minority youngsters. Extensive knowledge of bilingual, ESL, and English-only programs is essential in order to provide each child with the best possible educational setting.

When a non-English-speaking child crosses the threshold into the classroom, it should be reassuring to the teacher that the child learned his first language without much difficulty and that learning the second language is achieved in much the same way. All the teacher really needs to know are some simple techniques suggested by the research. And most important, the teacher can be effective without knowing one single word of the child's primary language.

References

Bruner, J. "Vygotsky: A Historical and Conceptual Perspective." In *Culture, Communication, and Cognition: Vygotskian Perspectives,* edited by J. Wertsch. New York: Cambridge University Press, 1985.

Chomsky, N. *Language and Mind.* New York: Harcourt, Brace & World, 1968.

Cummins, J. "The Role of Primary Language Development in Promoting Educational Success for Language Minority Students." In *Schooling and Language Minority Students: A Theoretical Framework.* Sacramento: California State Department of Education, 1981.

Galyean, Beverly. "A Confluent Design for Language Teaching." *TESOL Quarterly* 11 (June 1977): 143-56.

Halliday, M. *Learning How to Mean.* New York: Elsvier North-Holand, 1975.

Hennings, D. *Communication in Action: Teaching the Language Arts.* Boston: Houghton Mifflin, 1983.

Johns, K., and Espinoza, C. *Mainstreaming Language Minority Children in Reading and Writing.* Fastback 340. Bloomington, Ind.: Phi Delta Kappa Educational Foundation, 1992.

Krashen, S.D., and Terrell, T.D. *The Natural Approach: Language Acquisition in the Classroom.* San Francisco: Alemany, 1983.

Snow, M.A.; Met, M.; and Genesee, F. "A Conceptual Framework for the Integration of Language and Content in

Second/Foreign Language Instruction." *TESOL Quarterly* 23, no. 2 (1989): 201-17.

Vygotsky, L. *Mind in Society: The Development of Psychological Processes.* Cambridge, Mass.: Harvard University Press, 1978.

Recent Books Published by the
Phi Delta Kappa Educational Foundation

100 Classic Books About Higher Education
C. Fincher, G. Keller, E.G. Bogue, and J. Thelin
Trade paperback. $29 (PDK members, $21.75)

**Whose Values? Reflections of a New England
Prep School Teacher**
Barbara Bernache-Baker
Cloth. $49 (PDK members, $38)
Trade paperback. $24 (PDK members, $18)

American Education in the 21st Century
Dan H. Wishnietsky
Trade paperback. $22 (PDK members, $16.50)

Readings on Leadership in Education
From the Archives of Phi Delta Kappa International
Trade paperback. $22 (PDK members, $16.50)

Profiles of Leadership in Education
Mark F. Goldberg
Trade paperback. $22 (PDK members, $16.50)

**Use Order Form on Next Page
Or Phone 1-800-766-1156**

*A processing charge is added to all orders.
Prices are subject to change without notice.*

Complete online catalog at http://www.pdkintl.org

Order Form

SHIP TO:

STREET

CITY/STATE OR PROVINCE/ZIP OR POSTAL CODE

DAYTIME PHONE NUMBER	PDK MEMBER ROLL NUMBER

QUANTITY	TITLE	PRICE

ORDERS MUST INCLUDE PROCESSING CHARGE

Total Merchandise	Processing Charge
Up to $50	$5
$50.01 to $100	$10
More than $100	$10 plus 5% of total

Special shipping available upon request.
Prices subject to change without notice.

SUBTOTAL	
Indiana residents add 5% Sales Tax	
PROCESSING CHARGE	
TOTAL	

☐ Payment Enclosed (check payable to Phi Delta Kappa International)

Bill my   ☐ VISA   ☐ MasterCard   ☐ American Express   ☐ Discover

ACCT #   DATE

EXP DATE   SIGNATURE

Mail or fax your order to: Phi Delta Kappa International,
P.O. Box 789, Bloomington, IN 47402-0789. USA
Fax: (812) 339-0018. Phone: (812) 339-1156

**For fastest service, phone 1-800-766-1156
and use your credit card.**